A Detai

Mediterranean Diet

Cookbook

Quick and Easy Mediterranean Diet Cookbook
will help you learn all the basics to get started and
maintain this healthy lifestyle

Jose Murphy

Table of Contents

question by the reader will render any resulting actions solely under their purview. There are no scenarios in which the publisher or the original author of this work can be in any fashion deemed liable for any hardship or damages that may befall them after undertaking information described herein.

Additionally, the information in the following pages is intended only for informational purposes and should thus be thought of as universal. As befitting its nature, it is presented without assurance regarding its prolonged validity or interim quality. Trademarks that are mentioned are done without written consent and can in no way be considered an endorsement from the trademark holder.

INTRODUCTION

The Mediterranean eating regimen is a way of life. It's a method of eating so as to carry on with a full and solid life. When following along these lines of eating you'll get in shape, yet you'll likewise reinforce your heart and give your body all the best possible supplements important to carry on with a long and profitable life. Individuals following the Mediterranean eating regimen have been connected to a lower danger of Alzheimer's malady and malignancy, better generally speaking cardiovascular wellbeing, and an all-inclusive life expectancy. A Mediterranean style eating regimen is joined by a way of life. The way of life has many things that complete the eating routine. It incorporates a lot of exercise, not smoking, drinking in moderation, and having an enthusiasm for your family and life. This is a genuinely effective methodology for keeping up a solid life. The basic premise of this eating routine is that you eat a considerable measure of vegetables, fruits, cereals, nuts, and whole grains. You eat fish or meat scarcely. The omission of meat lessens your hazard of malignancy. You eat some bread. These are a few of the fundamental things that this eating regimen is all about.

The other portion of the Mediterranean eating regimen is the social component. You eat with your loved ones, family, and companions. You profit by the nourishment that you get and you savor your life. You eat inwardly back and center. Your family and companions appreciate it and they likewise figure out how to appreciate it. You meet a few people who are like-minded and you progress toward becoming a family. You get to appreciate your life since you're living it to the most astounding extent conceivable.

You can't take in the Mediterranean eating routine truly unless you be mindful of the exercise, the moderation, and being with the individuals who make it an occurrence to appreciate life. This is for the most part an approach of life. In the event that you need to accomplish the full advantages let this be the best way you choose to live your life. For the most part the general public who are doing it go to the gatherings that are as a rule home based. They have fun, they do things under the sun, and they do issues with their families and clan. They make a decent attempt to live in that sort of setting as opposed to the conventional social environment that a great many people are ordinarily in.

The last piece of the Mediterranean eating regimen is the way of life. One of the things that can be exceptionally harming is the way that you don't chat with your folks sufficiently. You don't get yourself the chance to hear your companions talk about the things that they appreciate, the things that they comprehend, and the things that they be in a position to do for themselves. They appreciate listening to you talk approximately the things that you appreciate, the things that you comprehend, and the things that you can do for yourself. Planning an occasion to get together so you can talk with your companions about your most loved subjects and every one of the underlying intricacies of your life is an essential piece on the way to accomplish the full advantages of the Mediterranean eating routine.

SMOOTHIES AND DRINKS RECIPES

Almonds & Blueberries Smoothie

Preparation Time: 5 minutes

Cooking Time: 3 minutes

Servings: 2

Ingredients:

- 1/4 cup ground almonds, unsalted

- 1 cup fresh blueberries

- Fresh juice of a 1 lemon

- 1 cup fresh kale leaf

- 1/2 cup coconut water

- 1 cup water

- 2 tablespoon plain yogurt (optional)

Directions:

1. Dump all ingredients in your high-speed blender, and blend until your smoothie is smooth.

2. Pour the mixture in a chilled glass.

3. Serve and enjoy!

Nutrition: Calories: 110, Carbohydrates: 8g, Proteins: 2g, Fat: 7g, Fiber: 2g,

Almonds and Zucchini Smoothie

Preparation Time: 5 minutes

Cooking Time: 3 minutes

Servings: 2

Ingredients:

- 1 cup zucchini, cooked and mashed - unsalted

- 1 1/2 cups almond milk

- 1 tablespoon almond butter (plain, unsalted)

- 1 teaspoon pure almond extract

- 2 tablespoon ground almonds or macadamia almonds

- 1/2 cup water

- 1 cup ice cubes crushed (optional, for serving)

Directions:

1. Dump all ingredients from the list above in your fast-speed blender; blend for 45 - 60 seconds or to taste.

2. Serve with crushed ice.

Nutrition: Calories: 322, Carbohydrates: 6g, Proteins: 6g, Fat: 30g, Fiber: 3.5g

Avocado with Walnut Butter Smoothie

Preparation Time: 5 minutes

Cooking Time: 3 minutes

Servings: 2

Ingredients:

- 1 avocado (diced)

- 1 cup baby spinach

- 1 cup coconut milk (canned)

- 1 tablespoon walnut butter, unsalted

- 2 tablespoon natural sweetener such as stevia, erythritol, truvia...etc.

Directions:

1. Place all ingredients into food processor or a blender; blend until smooth or to taste.

2. Add more or less walnut butter.

3. Drink and enjoy!

Nutrition: Calories: 364, Carbohydrates: 7g, Proteins: 8g, Fat: 35g, Fiber: 5.5g

Baby Spinach and Dill Smoothie

Preparation Time: 5 minutes

Cooking Time: 3 minutes

Servings: 2

Ingredients:

- 1 cup of fresh baby spinach leaves

- 2 tablespoon of fresh dill, chopped

- 1 1/2 cup of water

- 1/2 avocado, chopped into cubes

- 1 tablespoon chia seeds (optional)

- 2 tablespoon of natural sweetener stevia or erythritol (optional)

Directions:

1. Place all ingredients into fast-speed blender. Beat until smooth and all ingredients united well.

2. Serve and enjoy!

Nutrition: Calories: 136, Carbohydrates: 8g, Proteins: 7g, Fat: 10g, Fiber: 9g

Blueberries and Coconut Smoothie

Preparation Time: 5 minutes

Cooking Time: 3 minutes

Servings: 5

Ingredients:

- 1 cup of frozen blueberries, unsweetened

- 1 cup stevia or erythritol sweetener

- 2 cups coconut milk (canned)

- 1 cup of fresh spinach leaves

- 2 tablespoon shredded coconut (unsweetened)

- 3/4 cup water

Directions:

1. Place all ingredients from the list in food-processor or in your strong blender.

2. Blend for 45 - 60 seconds or to taste.

3. Ready for drink! Serve!

Nutrition: Calories: 190, Carbohydrates: 8g, Proteins: 3g, Fat: 18g, Fiber: 2g,

Collard Greens and Cucumber Smoothie

Preparation Time: 15 minutes

Cooking Time: 5 minutes

Servings: 2

Ingredients:

- 1 cup collard greens

- A few fresh pepper mint leaves

- 1 big cucumber

- 1 lime, freshly juiced

- 1/2 cups avocado sliced

- 1 1/2 cup water

- 1 cup crushed ice

- 1/4 cup of natural sweetener erythritol or stevia (optional)

Directions:

1. Rinse and clean your collard greens from any dirt.

2. Blend all ingredients in a blender till your smoothie is combined well.

3. Pour in a glass and drink. Enjoy!

Nutrition: Calories: 123, Carbohydrates: 8g, Proteins: 4g, Fat: 11g, Fiber: 6g

Creamy Dandelion Greens and Celery Smoothie

Preparation Time: 10 minutes

Cooking Time: 3 minutes

Servings: 2

Ingredients:

- 1 handful of raw dandelion greens

- 2 celery sticks

- 2 tablespoon chia seeds

- 1 small piece of ginger, minced

- 1/2 cup almond milk

- 1/2 cup of water

- 1/2 cup plain yogurt

Directions:

1. Rinse and clean dandelion leaves from any dirt; add in a high-speed blender.

2. Clean the ginger; keep only inner part and cut in small slices; add in a blender.

3. Blend all remaining ingredients until smooth.

4. Serve and enjoy!

Nutrition: Calories: 58, Carbohydrates: 5g, Proteins: 3g, Fat: 6g, Fiber: 3g

Butter Pecan and Coconut Smoothie

Preparation Time: 5 minutes

Cooking Time: 2 minutes

Servings: 2

Ingredients:

- 1 cup coconut milk, canned

- 1 scoop butter pecan powdered creamer

- 2 cups fresh spinach leaves, chopped

- 1/2 banana frozen or fresh

- 2 tablespoon stevia granulated sweetener to taste

- 1/2 cup water

- 1 cup ice cubes crushed

Directions:

1. Place ingredients from the list above in your high-speed blender.

2. Blend for 35 - 50 seconds or until all ingredients combined well.

3. Add less or more crushed ice.

4. Drink and enjoy!

Nutrition: Calories: 268, Carbohydrates: 7g, Proteins: 6g, Fat: 26g, Fiber: 1.5g

Fresh Cucumber, Kale and Raspberry Smoothie

Preparation Time: 10 minutes

Cooking Time: 3 minutes

Servings: 3

Ingredients:

- 1 1/2 cups of cucumber, peeled

- 1/2 cup raw kale leaves

- 1 1/2 cups fresh raspberries

- 1 cup of almond milk

- 1 cup of water

- Ice cubes crushed (optional)

- 2 tablespoon natural sweetener (stevia, erythritol...etc.)

Directions:

1. Place all Ingredients listed in a High-Speed Blender; Blend For 35 - 40 Seconds.
2. Serve Into Chilled Glasses.
3. Add More Natural Sweeter if you like. Enjoy!

Nutrition: Calories: 70, Carbohydrates: 8g, Proteins: 3g, Fat: 6g, Fiber: 5g

Green Coconut Smoothie

Preparation Time: 10 minutes

Cooking Time: 3 minutes

Servings: 2

Ingredients:

- 1 1/4 cup coconut milk (canned)
- 2 tablespoon chia seeds
- 1 cup of fresh kale leaves
- 1 cup of spinach leaves
- 1 scoop vanilla Protein powder
- 1 cup ice cubes
- Granulated stevia sweetener (to taste; optional)
- 1/2 cup water

Directions:

1. Rinse and clean kale and the spinach leaves from any dirt.
2. Add all ingredients in your blender.
3. Blend until you get a nice smoothie
4. Serve into chilled glass.

Nutrition: Calories: 179, Carbohydrates: 5g, Proteins: 4g, Fat: 18g, Fiber: 2.5g

Blueberry Matcha Smoothie

Preparation Time: 5 minutes

Cooking Time: 0 minutes

Servings: 2

Ingredients:

- 2 Cups Blueberries, Frozen
- 2 Cups Almond Milk
- 1 Banana
- 2 Tablespoons Protein Powder, Optional
- ¼ Teaspoon Ground Cinnamon
- 1 Tablespoon Chia Seeds
- 1 Tablespoon Matcha Powder
- ¼ Teaspoon Ground Ginger
- A Pinch Sea Salt

Directions:

1. Blend everything until smooth.

Nutrition: Calories: 208 Protein: 8.7 Grams Fat: 5.7 Grams Carbs: 31 Grams

Pumpkin Pie Smoothie

Preparation Time: 5 minutes

Cooking Time: 0 minutes

Servings: 2

Ingredients:

- 1 Banana
- ½ Cup Pumpkin, Canned & Unsweetened
- 2-3 Ice Cubes
- 1 Cup Almond Milk
- 2 Tablespoons Almond Butter, Heaping
- 1 Teaspoon Ground Nutmeg
- 1 Teaspoon Ground Cinnamon
- 1 Teaspoon Vanilla Extract Pure
- 1 Teaspoon Maple Syrup, Pure

Directions:

1. Blend everything together until smooth.

Nutrition: Calories: 235 Protein: 5.6 Grams Fat: 11 Grams Carbs: 27.8 Grams

Fig Smoothie

Preparation Time: 5 minutes

Cooking Time: 0 minutes

Servings: 2

Ingredients:

- 7 Figs, Halved (Fresh or Frozen)
- 1 Banana
- 1 Cup Whole Milk Yogurt, Plain
- 1 Cup Almond Milk
- 1 Teaspoon Flaxseed, Ground
- 1 Tablespoon Almond Butter
- 1 Teaspoon Honey, Raw
- 3-4 Ice Cubes

Dircctions:

1. Blend all together ingredients until smooth, and serve immediately.

Nutrition: Calories: 362 Protein: 9 Grams Fat: 12 Grams Carbs: 60 Grams

Ginger, Carrot, and Turmeric Smoothie

Preparation Time: 5 minutes

Cooking Time: 0 minutes

Servings: 2

Ingredients:

- 1/8 tsp. Cayenne pepper
- 1 tsp. Turmeric, ground
- 1 tsp. Ginger, ground
- 1 tbsp. Hemp seeds, raw, shelled
- 1 cup Coconut water
- ½ cup Mango, fresh or frozen chunks
- 1 large Carrot, peeled and chopped
- 1 Orange, peeled and separated

Directions:

1. Puree all of the ingredients together with one-half cup of ice until smooth and drink immediately.

Nutrition: Calories 250 35 grams sugar 4.5 grams fat 7 grams fiber 48 grams carbs 6 grams protein

Kiwi Strawberry Smoothie

Preparation Time: 10 minutes

Cooking Time: 0 minutes

Servings: 1

Ingredients:

- 1 Kiwi, peeled and chopped
- ½ cup Strawberries, fresh or frozen, chopped
- 1 cup Milk, almond or coconut
- 1 tsp. Basil, ground
- 1 tsp. Turmeric, ground
- 1 Banana, diced
- ¼ cup Chia seed powder

Directions:

1. Drink immediately after all the ingredients have been well mixed.

Nutrition: Calories 250 9.9 grams sugar 1 gram fat 34 carbs grams 4.3 grams fiber

Blended Coconut Milk and Banana Breakfast Smoothie

Preparation Time: 10 minutes

Cooking Time: 0 minutes

Servings: 4

Ingredients:

- 4 ripe medium-sized bananas
- 4 tbsp. flax seeds
- 2 cups almond milk
- 2 cups coconut milk
- 4 tsp. cinnamon

Directions:

1. Peel the banana and slice it into ½-inch pieces. Put all the ingredients in the blender and blend into a smoothie. Add a dash of cinnamon at the top of the smoothie before serving.

Nutrition: Calories: 332 kcal Protein: 12.49 g Fat: 14.42 g Carbohydrates: 42.46 g

Kale Smoothie

Preparation Time: 10 minutes

Cooking Time: 0 minutes

Servings: 2

Ingredients:

- 10 kale leaves
- 5 bananas, peeled and cut into chunks
- 2 pears, chopped
- 5 tbsp. almond butter
- 5 cups almond milk

Directions:

1. In your blender, mix the kale with the bananas, pears, almond butter, and almond milk.
2. Pulse well, divide into glasses, and serve. Enjoy!

Nutrition: Calories: 267 Fat: 11 g Protein: 7 g Carbs: 15 g Fiber: 7 g

Raspberry Smoothie

Preparation Time: 10 minutes

Cooking Time: 0 minutes

Servings: 2

Ingredients:

- 1 avocado, pitted and peeled
- 3/4 cup raspberry juice
- 3/4 cup orange juice
- 1/2 cup raspberries

Directions:

1. In your blender, mix the avocado with the raspberry juice, orange juice, and raspberries.
2. Pulse well, divide into 2 glasses, and serve. Enjoy!

Nutrition: Calories: 125 Fat: 11 g Protein: 3 g Carbs: 9 g Fiber: 7 g

Pineapple Smoothie

Preparation Time: 10 minutes

Cooking Time: 0 minutes

Servings: 2

Ingredients:

- 1 cup coconut water
- 1 orange, peeled and cut into quarters
- 1 1/2 cups pineapple chunks
- 1 tbsp. fresh grated ginger
- 1 tsp. chia seeds
- 1 tsp. turmeric powder
- A pinch black pepper

Directions:

1. In your blender, mix the coconut water with the orange, pineapple, ginger, chia seeds, turmeric, and black pepper.
2. Pulse well, pour into a glass.
3. Serve for breakfast. Enjoy!

Nutrition: Calories: 151 Fat: 2 g Protein: 4 g Carbs: 12 g Fiber: 6 g

Beet Smoothie

Preparation Time: 10 minutes

Cooking Time: 0 minutes

Servings: 2

Ingredients:

- 10 oz. almond milk, unsweetened
- 2 beets, peeled and quartered
- 1/2 banana, peeled and frozen
- 1/2 cup cherries, pitted
- 1 tbsp. almond butter

Directions:

1. In your blender, mix the milk with the beets, banana, cherries, and butter.
2. Pulse well, pour into glasses, and serve. Enjoy!

Nutrition: Calories: 165 Fat: 5 g Protein: 5 g Carbs: 22 g Fiber: 6 g

Blueberry Smoothie

Preparation Time: 10 minutes

Cooking Time: 0 minutes

Servings: 1

Ingredients:

- 1 banana, peeled
- 2 handfuls baby spinach
- 1 tbsp. almond butter
- 1/2 cup blueberries
- 1/4 tsp. ground cinnamon
- 1 tsp. maca powder
- 1/2 cup water
- 1/2 cup almond milk, unsweetened

Directions:

1. In your blender, mix the spinach with the banana, blueberries, almond butter, cinnamon, maca powder, water, and milk.
2. Pulse well, pour into a glass, and serve. Enjoy!

Nutrition: Calories: 341 Fat: 12 g Protein: 10 g Carbs: 54 g Fiber: 12 g

Strawberry Oatmeal Smoothie

Preparation Time: 10 minutes

Cooking Time: 0 minutes

Servings: 1

Ingredients:

- 1 cup soy milk
- 1/2 cup rolled oats
- 1 banana, broken into chunks
- 14 frozen strawberries
- 1/2 tsp. vanilla extract
- 1 1/2 tsp. honey

Directions:

1. Add everything to a blender jug.
2. Cover the jug tightly.
3. Blend until smooth. Serve and enjoy!

Nutrition: Calories: 172 Fat: 0.4 g Protein: 5.6 g Carbs: 8 g Fiber: 2 g

Raspberry Banana Smoothie

Preparation Time: 10 minutes

Cooking Time: 0 minutes

Servings: 1

Ingredients:

- 1 banana
- 16 whole almonds
- 1/4 cup rolled oats
- 1 tbsp. flaxseed meal
- 1 cup frozen raspberries
- 1 cup raspberry yogurt
- 1/4 cup Concord grape juice
- 1 cup almond milk

Directions:

1. Add everything to a blender jug.
2. Cover the jug tightly.
3. Blend until smooth and then serve. Enjoy!

Nutrition: Calories: 214 Fat: 0.4 g Protein: 5.6 g Carbs: 8 g Fiber: 2.3 g

Almond Blueberry Smoothie

Preparation Time: 10 minutes

Cooking Time: 0 minutes

Servings: 1

Ingredients:

- 1 cup frozen blueberries
- 1 banana
- 1/2 cup almond milk
- 1 tbsp. almond butter
- Water, as needed

Directions:

1. Add everything to a blender jug.
2. Cover the jug tightly.
3. Blend until smooth. Serve and enjoy!

Nutrition: Calories: 211 Fat: 0.2 g Protein: 5.6 g Carbs: 3.4 g Fiber: 2.3 g

Green Vanilla Smoothie

Preparation Time: 10 minutes

Cooking Time: 0 minutes

Servings: 1

Ingredients:

- 1 banana, cut in chunks
- 1 cup grapes
- 1 tub (6 oz.) vanilla yogurt
- 1/2 apple, cored and chopped
- 1 1/2 cups fresh spinach leaves

Directions:

1. Add everything to a blender jug.
2. Cover the jug tightly.
3. Blend until smooth. Serve and enjoy!

Nutrition: Calories: 131 Fat: 0.2 g Protein: 2.6 g Carbs: 9.1 g Fiber: 1.3 g

Purple Fruit Smoothie

Preparation Time: 10 minutes

Cooking Time: 0 minutes

Servings: 1

Ingredients:

- 2 frozen bananas, cut in chunks
- 1/2 cup frozen blueberries
- 1 cup orange juice
- 1 tbsp. honey, optional
- 1 tsp. vanilla extract, optional

Directions:

1. Add everything to a blender jug.
2. Cover the jug tightly.
3. Blend until smooth. Serve and enjoy!

Nutrition: Calories: 133 Fat: 1.1 g Protein: 3.6 g Carbs: 7.6 g Fiber: 1.3 g

Vanilla Avocado Smoothie

Preparation Time: 10 minutes

Cooking Time: 0 minutes

Servings: 1

Ingredients:

- 1 ripe avocado, halved and pitted
- 1 cup almond milk
- 1/2 cup vanilla yogurt
- 3 tbsp. honey
- 8 ice cubes

Directions:

1. Add everything to a blender jug.
2. Cover the jug tightly.
3. Blend until smooth. Serve and enjoy!

Nutrition: Calories: 143 Fat: 1.2 g Protein: 4.6 g Carbs: 21 g Fiber: 2.3 g

Triple Fruit Smoothie

Preparation Time: 10 minutes

Cooking Time: 0 minutes

Servings: 1

Ingredients:

- 1 kiwi, sliced
- 1 banana, peeled and chopped
- 1/2 cup blueberries
- 1 cup strawberries
- 1 cup ice cubes
- 1/2 cup orange juice
- 1 container (8 oz.) peach yogurt

Directions:

1. Add everything to a blender jug
2. Cover the jug tightly.
3. Blend until smooth. Serve and enjoy!

Nutrition: Calories: 124 Fat: 0.4 g Protein: 5.6 g Carbs: 8 g Fiber: 2.3 g

Peach Maple Smoothie

Preparation Time: 10 minutes

Cooking Time: 0 minutes

Servings: 1

Ingredients:

- 4 large peaches, peeled and chopped
- 2 tbsp. maple syrup
- 1 cup fat-free yogurt
- 1 cup ice

Directions:

1. Add everything to a blender jug.
2. Cover the jug tightly.
3. Blend until smooth. Serve and enjoy!

Nutrition: Calories: 125 Fat: 0.4 g Protein: 5.6 g Carbs: 8 g Fiber: 2.3 g

Pink California Smoothie

Preparation Time: 10 minutes

Cooking Time: 0 minutes

Servings: 1

Ingredients:

- 7 large strawberries
- 1 container (8 oz.) lemon yogurt
- 1/3 cup orange juice

Direction:

1. Add everything to a blender jug.
2. Cover the jug tightly.
3. Blend until smooth. Serve and enjoy!

Nutrition: Calories: 144 Fat: 0.4 g Protein: 5.6 g Carbs: 8 g Fiber: 2.3 g

Carrot and Orange Turmeric Drink

Preparation Time: 5 minutes

Cooking Time: 0 minutes

Servings: 2

Ingredients:

- 2 carrots, peeled, chopped
- 1 cup orange juice
- 1/2 inch ginger slice
- 2 tbsp. sugar
- 1 tbsp. lemon juice
- 1/4 tsp. turmeric powder

Direction:

1. In a blender, add orange juice, sugar, turmeric powder, carrots, and lemon juice. Blend well.
2. Pour into serving glasses. Serve and enjoy!

Nutrition: Calories: 153 kcal Protein: 4.47 g Fat: 3.3 g Carbohydrates: 27.02 g

carrot citrus

Voluptuous Vanilla Hot Drink

Preparation Time: 10 minutes

Cooking Time: 0 minutes

Servings: 1

Ingredients:

- 3 cups unsweetened almond milk (or 1 1/2 cup full-fat coconut milk + 1 1/2 cups
- water)
- Stevia to taste
- 1 scoop of hemp protein
- 1/2 Tbsp. ground cinnamon (or more to taste)
- 1/2 Tbsp. vanilla extract

Directions:

1. Place the almond milk into a pitcher. Place ground cinnamon, hemp, vanilla extract in a small saucepan over medium-high heat. Heat until the pure liquid stevia is just melted and then pour the pure liquid stevia mixture into the pitcher.
2. Stir until the pure liquid stevia is well combined with the almond milk. Bring the pitcher in the fridge and allow to chill for at least two hours. Stir well before serving.

Nutrition: Calories: 656 kcal Protein: 42.12 g Fat: 33.05 g Carbohydrates: 44.45 g

SEAFOOD RECIPES

Baked Bean Fish Meal

Preparation Time: 10 minutes

Cooking Time: 10 minutes

Servings: 4

Size/ Portion: 1 ounce

Ingredients:

- 1 tablespoon balsamic vinegar

- 2 ½ cups green beans

- 1-pint cherry or grape tomatoes

- 4 (4 ounce each) fish fillets, such as cod or tilapia

- 2 tablespoons olive oil

Directions:

1. Preheat an oven to 400 degrees. Grease two baking sheets with some olive oil or olive oil spray. Arrange 2 fish fillets on each sheet. In a mixing bowl, pour olive oil and vinegar. Combine to mix well with each other.

2. Mix green beans and tomatoes. Combine to mix well with each other. Combine both mixtures well with each other. Add mixture equally over fish fillets. Bake for 6-8 minutes, until fish opaque and easy to flake. Serve warm.

Nutrition: 229 Calories 13g Fat 2.5g Protein

Mushroom Cod Stew

Preparation Time: 10 minutes

Cooking Time: 20 minutes

Servings: 6

Size/ Portion: 2 cups

Ingredients:

- 2 tablespoons extra-virgin olive oil
- 2 garlic cloves, minced
- 1 can tomato
- 2 cups chopped onion
- ¾ teaspoon smoked paprika
- a (12-ounce) jar roasted red peppers
- 1/3 cup dry red wine
- ¼ teaspoon kosher or sea salt
- ¼ teaspoon black pepper
- 1 cup black olives
- 1 ½ pounds cod fillets, cut into 1-inch pieces
- 3 cups sliced mushrooms

Directions:

1. Get medium-large cooking pot, warm up oil over medium heat. Add onions and stir-cook for 4 minutes.

2. Add garlic and smoked paprika; cook for 1 minute, stirring often. Add tomatoes with juice, roasted peppers, olives, wine, pepper, and salt; stir gently.

3. Boil mixture. Add the cod and mushrooms; turn down heat to medium. Close and cook until the cod is easy to flake, stir in between. Serve warm.

Nutrition: 238 Calories 7g Fat 3.5g Protein

Spiced Swordfish

Preparation Time: 10 minutes

Cooking Time: 15 minutes

Servings: 4

Size/ Portion: 7 ounces

Ingredients:

- 4 (7 ounces each) swordfish steaks
- 1/2 teaspoon ground black pepper
- 12 cloves of garlic, peeled
- 3/4 teaspoon salt
- 1 1/2 teaspoon ground cumin
- 1 teaspoon paprika
- 1 teaspoon coriander
- 3 tablespoons lemon juice
- 1/3 cup olive oil

Directions:

1. Take a blender or food processor, open the lid and add all the ingredients except for swordfish. Close the lid and blend to make a smooth mixture. Pat dry fish steaks; coat evenly with the prepared spice mixture.

2. Add them over an aluminum foil, cover and refrigerator for 1 hour. Preheat a griddle pan over high heat, pour oil and heat it. Add fish steaks; stir-cook for 5-6 minutes per side until cooked through and evenly browned. Serve warm.

Nutrition: 255 Calories 12g Fat 0.5g Protein

grab your fork

Anchovy Pasta Mania

Preparation Time: 10 minutes

Cooking Time: 20 minutes

Servings: 4

Size/ Portion: 1 fillet

Ingredients:

- 4 anchovy fillets, packed in olive oil
- ½ pound broccoli, cut into 1-inch florets
- 2 cloves garlic, sliced
- 1-pound whole-wheat penne
- 2 tablespoons olive oil
- ¼ cup Parmesan cheese, grated
- Salt and black pepper, to taste
- Red pepper flakes, to taste

Directions:

1. Cook pasta as directed over pack; drain and set aside. Take a medium saucepan or skillet, add oil. Heat over medium heat.

2. Add anchovies, broccoli, and garlic, and stir-cook until veggies turn tender for 4-5 minutes. Take off heat; mix in the pasta. Serve warm with Parmesan

cheese, red pepper flakes, salt, and black pepper sprinkled on top.

Nutrition: 328 Calories 8g Fat 7g Protein

Shrimp Garlic Pasta

Preparation Time: 10 minutes

Cooking Time: 15 minutes

Servings: 4

Size/ Portion: 2 ounces

Ingredients:

- 1-pound shrimp

- 3 garlic cloves, minced

- 1 onion, finely chopped

- 1 package whole wheat or bean pasta

- 4 tablespoons olive oil

- Salt and black pepper, to taste

- ¼ cup basil, cut into strips

- ¾ cup chicken broth, low-sodium

Directions:

1. Cook pasta as directed over pack; rinse and set aside. Get medium saucepan, add oil then warm up over medium heat. Add onion, garlic and stir-cook until become translucent and fragrant for 3 minutes.

2. Add shrimp, black pepper (ground) and salt; stir-cook for 3 minutes until shrimps are opaque. Add broth and simmer for 2-3 more minutes. Add pasta

in serving plates; add shrimp mixture over; serve warm with basil on top.

Nutrition: 605 Calories 17g Fat 19g Protein

Vinegar Honeyed Salmon

Preparation Time: 10 minutes

Cooking Time: 5 minutes

Servings: 4

Size/ Portion: 8 ounces

Ingredients:

- 4 (8-ounce) salmon filets

- 1/2 cup balsamic vinegar

- 1 tablespoon honey

- Black pepper and salt, to taste

- 1 tablespoon olive oil

Directions:

1. Combine honey and vinegar. Combine to mix well with each other.

2. Season fish fillets with the black pepper (ground) and sea salt; brush with honey glaze. Take a medium saucepan or skillet, add oil.

3. Heat over medium heat. Add salmon fillets and stir-cook until medium rare in center and lightly browned for 3-4 minutes per side. Serve warm.

Nutrition: 481 Calories 16g Fat 1.5g Protein

Orange Fish Meal

Preparation Time: 10 minutes

Cooking Time: 5 minutes

Servings: 4

Size/ Portion: 4 ounces

Ingredients:

- ¼ teaspoon kosher or sea salt

- 1 tablespoon extra-virgin olive oil

- 1 tablespoon orange juice

- 4 (4-ounce) tilapia fillets, with or without skin

- ¼ cup chopped red onion

- 1 avocado, pitted, skinned, and sliced

Directions:

1. Take a baking dish of 9-inch; add olive oil, orange juice, and salt. Combine well. Add fish fillets and coat well.

2. Add onions over fish fillets. Cover with a plastic wrap. Microwave for 3 minutes until fish is cooked well and easy to flake. Serve warm with sliced avocado on top.

Nutrition: 231 Calories 9g Fat 2.5g Protein

Shrimp Zoodles

Preparation Time: 10 minutes

Cooking Time: 5 minutes

Servings: 2

Size/ Portion: 2 ounces

Ingredients:

- 2 tablespoons chopped parsley

- 2 teaspoons minced garlic

- 1 teaspoon salt

- ½ teaspoon black pepper

- 2 medium zucchinis, spiralized

- 3/4 pounds medium shrimp, peeled & deveined

- 1 tablespoon olive oil

- 1 lemon, juiced and zested

Directions:

1. Take a medium saucepan or skillet, add oil, lemon juice, lemon zest. Heat over medium heat. Add shrimps and stir-cook 1 minute per side.

2. Sauté garlic and red pepper flakes for 1 more minute. Add Zoodles and stir gently; cook for 3 minutes until cooked to satisfaction. Season well, serve warm with parsley on top.

Nutrition: 329 Calories 12g Fat 3g Protein

Asparagus Trout Meal

Preparation Time: 10 minutes

Cooking Time: 20 minutes

Servings: 4

Size/ Portion: ½ fillets

Ingredients:

- 2 pounds trout fillets
- 1-pound asparagus
- 1 tablespoon olive oil
- 1 garlic clove, finely minced
- 1 scallion, thinly sliced
- 4 medium golden potatoes
- 2 Roma tomatoes, chopped
- 8 pitted kalamata olives, chopped
- 1 large carrot, thinly sliced
- 2 tablespoons dried parsley
- ¼ cup ground cumin
- 2 tablespoons paprika
- 1 tablespoon vegetable bouillon seasoning
- ½ cup dry white wine

Directions:

1. In a mixing bowl, add fish fillets, white pepper and salt. Combine to mix well with each other. Take a medium saucepan or skillet, add oil.

2. Heat over medium heat. Add asparagus, potatoes, garlic, white part scallion, and stir-cook until become softened for 4-5 minutes. Add tomatoes, carrot and olives; stir-cook for 6-7 minutes until turn tender. Add cumin, paprika, parsley, bouillon seasoning, and salt. Stir mixture well.

3. Mix in white wine and fish fillets. Over low heat, cover and simmer mixture for about 6 minutes until fish is easy to flake, stir in between. Serve warm with green scallions on top.

Nutrition: 303 Calories 17g Fat 6g Protein

Kale Olive Tuna

Preparation Time: 10 minutes

Cooking Time: 15 minutes

Servings: 6

Size/ Portion: 1 ounce

Ingredients:

- 1 cup chopped onion

- 3 garlic cloves, minced

- 1 (2.25-ounce) can sliced olives

- 1-pound kale, chopped

- 3 tablespoons extra-virgin olive oil

- ¼ cup capers

- ¼ teaspoon crushed red pepper

- 2 teaspoons sugar

- 1 (15-ounce) can cannellini beans

- 2 (6-ounce) cans tuna in olive oil, un-drained

- ¼ teaspoon black pepper

- ¼ teaspoon kosher or sea salt

Directions:

1. Soak kale in boiling water for 2 minutes; drain and set aside. Take a medium-large cooking pot or stock pot, heat oil over medium heat.

2. Add onion and stir-cook until become translucent and softened. Add garlic and stir-cook until become fragrant for 1 minute.

3. Add olives, capers, and red pepper, and stir-cook for 1 minute. Mix in cooked kale and sugar. Over low heat, cover and simmer mixture for about 8-10 minutes, stir in between.

4. Add tuna, beans, pepper, and salt. Stir well and serve warm.

Nutrition: 242 Calories 11g Fat 7g Protein

Tangy Rosemary Shrimps

Preparation Time: 10 minutes

Cooking Time: 10 minutes

Servings: 6

Size/ Portion: ¼ ounce

Ingredients:

- 1 large orange, zested and peeled

- 3 garlic cloves, minced

- 1 ½ pounds raw shrimp, shells and tails removed

- 3 tablespoons olive oil

- 1 tablespoon chopped thyme

- 1 tablespoon chopped rosemary

- ¼ teaspoon black pepper

- ¼ teaspoon kosher or sea salt

Directions:

1. Take a zip-top plastic bag, add orange zest, shrimps, 2 tablespoons olive oil, garlic, thyme, rosemary, salt, and black pepper. Shake well and set aside to marinate for 5 minutes.

2. Take a medium saucepan or skillet, add 1 tablespoon olive oil. Heat over medium heat. Add shrimps and

stir-cook for 2-3 minutes per side until totally pink and opaque.

3. Slice orange into bite-sized wedges and add in a serving plate. Add shrimps and combine well. Serve fresh.

Nutrition: 187 Calories 7g Fat 0.5g Protein

Asparagus Salmon

Preparation Time: 10 minutes

Cooking Time: 15 minutes

Servings: 2

Size/ Portion: 1 fillet

Ingredients:

- 8.8-ounce bunch asparagus
- 2 small salmon fillets
- 1 ½ teaspoon salt
- 1 teaspoon black pepper
- 1 tablespoon olive oil
- 1 cup hollandaise sauce, low-carb

Directions:

1. Season well the salmon fillets. Take a medium saucepan or skillet, add oil. Heat over medium heat.

2. Add salmon fillets and stir-cook until evenly seared and cooked well for 4-5 minutes per side. Add asparagus and stir cook for 4-5 more minutes. Serve warm with hollandaise sauce on top.

Nutrition: 565 Calories 7g Fat 2.5g Protein

Tuna Nutty Salad

Preparation Time: 10 minutes

Cooking Time: 0 minutes

Servings: 4

Size/ Portion: 2 ounces

Ingredients:

- 1 tablespoon chopped tarragon

- 1 stalk celery, trimmed and finely diced

- 1 medium shallot, diced

- 3 tablespoons chopped chives

- 1 (5-ounce) can tuna (covered in olive oil)

- 1 teaspoon Dijon mustard

- 2-3 tablespoons mayonnaise

- 1/4 teaspoon salt

- 1/8 teaspoon pepper

- 1/4 cup pine nuts, toasted

Directions:

1. In a large salad bowl, add tuna, shallot, chives, tarragon, and celery. Combine to mix well with each other. In a mixing bowl, add mayonnaise, mustard, salt, and black pepper.

2. Combine to mix well with each other. Add mayonnaise mixture to salad bowl; toss well to combine. Add pine nuts and toss again. Serve fresh.

Nutrition: 236 Calories 14g Fat 1g Protein

Creamy Shrimp Soup

Preparation Time: 10 minutes

Cooking Time: 35 minutes

Servings: 6

Size/ Portion: 2 cups

Ingredients:

- 1-pound medium shrimp

- 1 leek, both whites and light green parts, sliced

- 1 medium fennel bulb, chopped

- 2 tablespoons olive oil

- 3 stalks celery, chopped

- 1 clove garlic, minced

- Sea salt and ground pepper to taste

- 4 cups vegetable or chicken broth

- 1 tablespoon fennel seeds

- 2 tablespoons light cream

- Juice of 1 lemon

Directions:

1. Take a medium-large cooking pot or Dutch oven, heat oil over medium heat. Add celery, leek, and fennel and stir-cook for about 15 minutes, until

---

vegetables are softened and browned. Add garlic; season with black pepper and sea salt to taste. Add fennel seed and stir.

2. Pour broth and bring to a boil. Over low heat, simmer mixture for about 20 minutes, stir in between. Add shrimp and cook until just pink for 3 minutes. Mix in cream and lemon juice; serve warm.

Nutrition: 174 Calories 5g Fat 2g Protein

Spiced Salmon with Vegetable Quinoa

Preparation Time: 30 minutes

Cooking Time: 10 minutes

Servings: 4

Size/ Portion: 5 ounces

Ingredients:

- 1 cup uncooked quinoa

- 1 teaspoon of salt, divided in half

- ¾ cup cucumbers, seeds removed, diced

- 1 cup of cherry tomatoes, halved

- ¼ cup red onion, minced

- 4 fresh basil leaves, cut in thin slices

- Zest from one lemon

- ¼ teaspoon black pepper

- 1 teaspoon cumin

- ½ teaspoon paprika

- 4 (5-oz.) salmon fillets

- 8 lemon wedges

- ¼ cup fresh parsley, chopped

Directions:

1. To a medium-sized saucepan, add the quinoa, 2 cups of water, and ½ teaspoons of the salt. Heat these until the water is boiling, then lower the temperature until it is simmering. Cover the pan and let it cook 20 minutes or as long as the quinoa package instructs. Turn off the burner under the quinoa and allow it to sit, covered, for at least another 5 minutes before serving.

2. Right before serving, add the onion, tomatoes, cucumbers, basil leaves, and lemon zest to the quinoa and use a spoon to stir everything together gently. In the meantime (while the quinoa cooks), prepare the salmon. Turn on the oven broiler to high and make sure a rack is in the lower part of the oven. To a small bowl, add the following components: black pepper, ½ teaspoon of the salt, cumin, and paprika. Stir them together.

3. Place foil over the top of a glass or aluminum baking sheet, then spray it with nonstick cooking spray. Place salmon fillets on the foil. Rub the spice mixture over each fillet (about ½ teaspoons of the spice mixture per fillet). Add the lemon wedges to the pan edges near the salmon.

4. Cook the salmon under the broiler for 8-10 minutes. Your goal is for the salmon to flake apart easily with a fork. Sprinkle the salmon with the parsley, then serve it with the lemon wedges and vegetable parsley. Enjoy!

Nutrition: 385 Calories 12.5g Fat 35.5g Protein

Baked Cod with Vegetables

Preparation Time: 15 minutes

Cooking Time: 25 minutes

Serving: 2

Size/ Portion: 2 pieces

Ingredients:

- 1 pound (454 g) thick cod fillet, cut into 4 even portions

- ¼ teaspoon onion powder (optional)

- ¼ teaspoon paprika

- 3 tablespoons extra-virgin olive oil

- 4 medium scallions

- ½ cup fresh chopped basil, divided

- 3 tablespoons minced garlic (optional)

- 2 teaspoons salt

- 2 teaspoons freshly ground black pepper

- ¼ teaspoon dry marjoram (optional)

- 6 sun-dried tomato slices

- ½ cup dry white wine

- ½ cup crumbled feta cheese

- 1 (15-ounce / 425-g) can oil-packed artichoke hearts, drained

- 1 lemon, sliced

- 1 cup pitted kalamata olives

- 1 teaspoon capers (optional)

- 4 small red potatoes, quartered

Direction:

1. Set oven to 375°F (190°C).

2. Season the fish with paprika and onion powder (if desired).

3. Heat an ovenproof skillet over medium heat and sear the top side of the cod for about 1 minute until golden. Set aside.

4. Heat the olive oil in the same skillet over medium heat. Add the scallions, ¼ cup of basil, garlic (if desired), salt, pepper, marjoram (if desired), tomato slices, and white wine and stir to combine. Boil then removes from heat.

5. Evenly spread the sauce on the bottom of skillet. Place the cod on top of the tomato basil sauce and scatter with feta cheese. Place the artichokes in the skillet and top with the lemon slices.

6. Scatter with the olives, capers (if desired), and the remaining ¼ cup of basil. Pullout from the heat and transfer to the preheated oven. Bake for 15 to 20 minutes

---

7. Meanwhile, place the quartered potatoes on a baking sheet or wrapped in aluminum foil. Bake in the oven for 15 minutes.

8. Cool for 5 minutes before serving.

Nutrition: 1168 calories 60g fat 64g protein

Slow Cooker Salmon in Foil

Preparation Time: 5 minutes

Cooking Time: 2 hours

Serving: 2

Size/ Portion: 6 ounces

Ingredients:

- 2 (6-ounce / 170-g) salmon fillets

- 1 tablespoon olive oil

- 2 cloves garlic, minced

- ½ tablespoon lime juice

- 1 teaspoon finely chopped fresh parsley

- ¼ teaspoon black pepper

Direction

1. Spread a length of foil onto a work surface and place the salmon fillets in the middle.

2. Blend olive oil, garlic, lime juice, parsley, and black pepper. Brush the mixture over the fillets. Fold the foil over and crimp the sides to make a packet.

3. Place the packet into the slow cooker, cover, and cook on High for 2 hours

4. Serve hot.

Nutrition: 446 calories 21g fat 65g protein

Dill Chutney Salmon

Preparation Time: 5 minutes

Cooking Time: 3 minutes

Serving: 2

Size/ Portion: 1 fillet

Ingredients:

Chutney:

- ¼ cup fresh dill
- ¼ cup extra virgin olive oil
- Juice from ½ lemon
- Sea salt, to taste

Fish:

- 2 cups water
- 2 salmon fillets
- Juice from ½ lemon
- ¼ teaspoon paprika
- Salt and freshly ground pepper to taste

Direction:

1. Pulse all the chutney ingredients in a food processor until creamy. Set aside.

2. Add the water and steamer basket to the Instant Pot. Place salmon fillets, skin-side down, on the steamer basket. Drizzle the lemon juice over salmon and sprinkle with the paprika.

3. Secure the lid. Select the Manual mode and set the cooking time for 3 minutes at High Pressure.

4. Once cooking is complete, do a quick pressure release. Carefully open the lid.

5. Season the fillets with pepper and salt to taste. Serve topped with the dill chutney.

Nutrition: 636 calories 41g fat 65g protein

Garlic-Butter Parmesan Salmon and Asparagus

Preparation Time: 10 minutes

Cooking Time: 15 minutes

Serving: 2

Size/ Portion: 1 fillet

Ingredients:

- 2 (6-ounce / 170-g) salmon fillets, skin on and patted dry

- Pink Himalayan salt

- Freshly ground black pepper, to taste

- 1 pound (454 g) fresh asparagus, ends snapped off

- 3 tablespoons almond butter

- 2 garlic cloves, minced

- ¼ cup grated Parmesan cheese

Direction:

1. Prep oven to 400°F (205°C). Line a baking sheet with aluminum foil.

2. Season both sides of the salmon fillets.

3. Situate salmon in the middle of the baking sheet and arrange the asparagus around the salmon.

4. Heat the almond butter in a small saucepan over medium heat.

5. Cook minced garlic

6. Drizzle the garlic-butter sauce over the salmon and asparagus and scatter the Parmesan cheese on top.

7. Bake in the preheated oven for about 12 minutes. You can switch the oven to broil at the end of cooking time for about 3 minutes to get a nice char on the asparagus.

8. Let cool for 5 minutes before serving.

Nutrition: 435 calories 26g fat 42g protein

Lemon Rosemary Roasted Branzino

Preparation Time: 15 minutes

Cooking Time: 30 minutes

Serving: 2

Size/ Portion: 1 fillet

Ingredients:

- 4 tablespoons extra-virgin olive oil, divided

- 2 (8-ounce) Branzino fillets

- 1 garlic clove, minced

- 1 bunch scallions

- 10 to 12 small cherry tomatoes, halved

- 1 large carrot, cut into ¼-inch rounds

- ½ cup dry white wine

- 2 tablespoons paprika

- 2 teaspoons kosher salt

- ½ tablespoon ground chili pepper

- 2 rosemary sprigs or 1 tablespoon dried rosemary

- 1 small lemon, thinly sliced

- ½ cup sliced pitted kalamata olives

Direction:

1. Heat a large ovenproof skillet over high heat until hot, about 2 minutes. Add 1 tablespoon of olive oil and heat

2. Add the Branzino fillets, skin-side up, and sear for 2 minutes. Flip the fillets and cook. Set aside.

3. Swirl 2 tablespoons of olive oil around the skillet to coat evenly.

4. Add the garlic, scallions, tomatoes, and carrot, and sauté for 5 minutes

5. Add the wine, stirring until all ingredients are well combined. Carefully place the fish over the sauce.

6. Preheat the oven to 450°F (235°C).

7. Brush the fillets with the remaining 1 tablespoon of olive oil and season with paprika, salt, and chili pepper. Top each fillet with a rosemary sprig and lemon slices. Scatter the olives over fish and around the skillet.

8. Roast for about 10 minutes until the lemon slices are browned. Serve hot.

Nutrition: 724 calories 43g fat 57g protein

Grilled Lemon Pesto Salmon

Preparation Time: 5 minutes

Cooking Time: 10 minutes

Serving: 2

Size/ Portion: 5 ounces

Ingredients:

- 10 ounces (283 g) salmon fillet

- 2 tablespoons prepared pesto sauce

- 1 large fresh lemon, sliced

- Cooking spray

Direction:

1. Preheat the grill to medium-high heat. Spray the grill grates with cooking spray.

2. Season the salmon well. Spread the pesto sauce on top.

3. Make a bed of fresh lemon slices about the same size as the salmon fillet on the hot grill, and place the salmon on top of the lemon slices. Put any additional lemon slices on top of the salmon.

4. Grill the salmon for 10 minutes.

5. Serve hot.

Nutrition: 316 calories 21g fat 29g protein

Steamed Trout with Lemon Herb Crust

Preparation Time: 10 minutes

Cooking Time: 15 minutes

Serving: 2

Size/ Portion: 1 piece

Ingredients:

- 3 tablespoons olive oil

- 3 garlic cloves, chopped

- 2 tablespoons fresh lemon juice

- 1 tablespoon chopped fresh mint

- 1 tablespoon chopped fresh parsley

- ¼ teaspoon dried ground thyme

- 1 teaspoon sea salt

- 1 pound (454 g) fresh trout (2 pieces)

- 2 cups fish stock

Direction:

1. Blend olive oil, garlic, lemon juice, mint, parsley, thyme, and salt. Brush the marinade onto the fish.

2. Insert a trivet in the Instant Pot. Fill in the fish stock and place the fish on the trivet.

3. Secure the lid. Select the Steam mode and set the cooking time for 15 minutes at High Pressure.

4. Once cooking is complete, do a quick pressure release. Carefully open the lid. Serve warm.

Nutrition: 477 calories 30g fat 52g protein

Roasted Trout Stuffed with Veggies

Preparation Time: 10 minutes

Cooking Time: 25 minutes

Serving: 2

Size/ Portion: 8 ounces

Ingredient:

- 2 (8-ounce) whole trout fillets
- 1 tablespoon extra-virgin olive oil
- ¼ teaspoon salt
- 1/8 teaspoon black pepper
- 1 small onion, thinly sliced
- ½ red bell pepper
- 1 poblano pepper
- 2 or 3 shiitake mushrooms, sliced
- 1 lemon, sliced

Direction:

1. Set oven to 425°F (220°C). Coat baking sheet with nonstick cooking spray.

2. Rub both trout fillets, inside and out, with the olive oil. Season with salt and pepper.

3. Mix together the onion, bell pepper, poblano pepper, and mushrooms in a large bowl. Stuff half of this mix into the cavity of each fillet. Top the mixture with 2 or 3 lemon slices inside each fillet.

4. Place the fish on the prepared baking sheet side by side. Roast in the preheated oven for 25 minutes

5. Pullout from the oven and serve on a plate.

Nutrition: 453 calories 22g fat 49g protein

Lemony Trout with Caramelized Shallots

Preparation Time: 10 minutes

Cooking Time: 20 minutes

Serving: 2

Size/ Portion: 4 ounces

Ingredients:

Shallots:

- 1 teaspoon almond butter
- 2 shallots, thinly sliced
- Dash salt

Trout:

- 1 tablespoon almond butter
- 2 (4-ounce / 113-g) trout fillets
- 3 tablespoons capers
- ¼ cup freshly squeezed lemon juice
- ¼ teaspoon salt
- Dash freshly ground black pepper
- 1 lemon, thinly sliced

Direction:

For Shallots

1. Situate skillet over medium heat, cook the butter, shallots, and salt for 20 minutes, stirring every 5 minutes.

For Trout

2. Meanwhile, in another large skillet over medium heat, heat 1 teaspoon of almond butter.

3. Add the trout fillets and cook each side for 3 minutes, or until flaky. Transfer to a plate and set aside.

4. In the skillet used for the trout, stir in the capers, lemon juice, salt, and pepper, then bring to a simmer. Whisk in the remaining 1 tablespoon of almond butter. Spoon the sauce over the fish.

5. Garnish the fish with the lemon slices and caramelized shallots before serving.

Nutrition: 344 calories 18g fat 21g protein

Easy Tomato Tuna Melts

Preparation Time: 5 minutes

Cooking Time: 4 minutes

Serving: 2

Size/ Portion: 2.5 ounces

Ingredients:

- 1 (5-oz) can chunk light tuna packed in water
- 2 tablespoons plain Greek yogurt
- 2 tablespoons finely chopped celery
- 1 tablespoon finely chopped red onion
- 2 teaspoons freshly squeezed lemon juice
- 1 large tomato, cut into ¾-inch-thick rounds
- ½ cup shredded Cheddar cheese

Direction:

1. Preheat the broiler to High.

2. Stir together the tuna, yogurt, celery, red onion, lemon juice, and cayenne pepper in a medium bowl.

3. Place the tomato rounds on a baking sheet. Top each with some tuna salad and Cheddar cheese.

4. Broil for 3 to 4 minutes until the cheese is melted and bubbly. Cool for 5 minutes before serving.

Nutrition: 244 calories 10g fat 30g protein

Mackerel and Green Bean Salad

Preparation Time: 10 minutes

Cooking Time: 10 minutes

Serving: 2

Size/ Portion: 2 cups

Ingredients:

- 2 cups green beans
- 1 tablespoon avocado oil
- 2 mackerel fillets
- 4 cups mixed salad greens
- 2 hard-boiled eggs, sliced
- 1 avocado, sliced
- 2 tablespoons lemon juice
- 2 tablespoons olive oil
- 1 teaspoon Dijon mustard
- Salt and black pepper, to taste

Direction:

1. Cook the green beans in pot of boiling water for about 3 minutes. Drain and set aside.

2. Melt the avocado oil in a pan over medium heat. Add the mackerel fillets and cook each side for 4 minutes.

3. Divide the greens between two salad bowls. Top with the mackerel, sliced egg, and avocado slices.

4. Scourge lemon juice, olive oil, mustard, salt, and pepper, and drizzle over the salad. Add the cooked green beans and toss to combine, then serve.

Nutrition: 737 calories 57g fat 34g protein

Hazelnut Crusted Sea Bass

Preparation Time: 10 minutes

Cooking Time: 15 minutes

Serving: 2

Size/ Portion: 1 fillet

Ingredients:

- 2 tablespoons almond butter

- 2 sea bass fillets

- 1/3 cup roasted hazelnuts

- A pinch of cayenne pepper

Direction

1. Ready oven to 425°F (220°C). Line a baking dish with waxed paper.

2. Brush the almond butter over the fillets.

3. Pulse the hazelnuts and cayenne in a food processor. Coat the sea bass with the hazelnut mixture, then transfer to the baking dish.

4. Bake in the preheated oven for about 15 minutes. Cool for 5 minutes before serving.

Nutrition: 468 calories 31g fat 40g protein

Shrimp and Pea Paella

Preparation Time: 20 minutes

Cooking Time: 60 minutes

Serving: 2

Size/ Portion: 4 ounces

Ingredients:

- 2 tablespoons olive oil
- 1 garlic clove, minced
- ½ large onion, minced
- 1 cup diced tomato
- ½ cup short-grain rice
- ½ teaspoon sweet paprika
- ½ cup dry white wine
- 1¼ cups low-sodium chicken stock
- 8 ounces (227 g) large raw shrimp
- 1 cup frozen peas
- ¼ cup jarred roasted red peppers

Direction

1. Heat the olive oil in a large skillet over medium-high heat.

2. Add the garlic and onion and sauté for 3 minutes, or until the onion is softened.

3. Add the tomato, rice, and paprika and stir for 3 minutes to toast the rice.

4. Add the wine and chicken stock and stir to combine. Bring the mixture to a boil.

5. Cover and set heat to medium-low, and simmer for 45 minutes

6. Add the shrimp, peas, and roasted red peppers. Cover and cook for an additional 5 minutes. Season with salt to taste and serve.

Nutrition: 646 calories 27g fat 42g protein

Conclusion

The Mediterranean diet considers various aspects of what "health" means. It does not just focus on what you eat but it also focuses on how you eat, who you eat with, and the activities you do in between eating. Each of these components can contribute to better health and a more fulfilling life. When we are lacking in any of these components, we tend to suffer from poor health, fatigue, depression and more. The Mediterranean diet was originally looked at because of its heart health benefits, but now it is clear to see that the traditional Mediterranean lifestyle from the 1950s was more than just a heart-healthy plan.

This book has helped you understand not only the benefits of this diet but has revealed effective tips and suggestions to help you transition into this type of diet. The changes can be made in small steps, because even the smallest change to shifting your diet to a more Mediterranean diet can have a whirlwind of benefits. You have learned how to swap the unhealthy foods you have been used to consuming with nutrient-dense and wholesome foods.

The Mediterranean diet is more than what you eat; it is a way of living. This diet reflects the true definition of what a diet should be. It encourages eating healthy nutritious foods, while also emphasizing the importance of physical activity and spending time with those we care about. The Mediterranean diet has been studied for decades and each time it seems a new benefit of this diet comes to light.

What needs to be done is adopting a new way of looking at food and mealtimes. Our world today stresses working harder and longer which means there is little time for enjoying meals. If we can change our perspective to see that the food, we eat is what makes us more efficient and productive, then we would be able to more easily change the way we eat.

This book has introduced you to what the Mediterranean diet is. It has helped you understand that this isn't your typical diet. That instead, the Mediterranean diet is about changing into a lifestyle that will bring you better health and happiness. This book has provided you with some of the findings from scientific research that supports the diet's benefits. You have learned that the diet consists of eating plenty of fresh fruits, vegetables, and healthy fats like extra virgin olive oil. You still have the freedom to indulge with brain-boosting fish, heart-healthy whole grains, and seafood and sporadically can enjoy a nice steak dinner. This diet is not limiting you to be mindful of your calorie intake or not to consume other important food groups.

The recipes in this book allow you to begin trying out delicious, flavorful, and healthy Mediterranean inspired meals. You have a number of breakfasts, lunch, and dinner options that are sure to satisfy and please everyone in your home. These recipes can be your starting point in taking control of your health.

You now have a better understanding that this diet is not about just losing weight. It is not a diet that allows you to eat your weight in pasta, or drink equal amounts of red wine. It has shown that you can use food as a form of natural medicine to reduce and eliminate the risk of many serious health conditions. You have learned how your food directly affects the way your body functions and when it is deprived of the nutrients it needs it will not be able to perform appropriately.

Now that you have all this information on how you can maintain and achieve optimal health, it is up to you to decide. Will you continue to choose a life where the foods you eat leads you down a road to illness and preventable suffering? Or will you make the change now to live your life and be the healthiest and happiest version of you? All you have to do is start with one small change and then go from